WITHDRAWN

# SOFTWARE DEVELOPMENT

SCIENCE • TECHNOLOGY • ENGINEERING

BY WIL MARA

CHILDREN'S PRESS®
An Imprint of Scholastic Inc.

CONTENT CONSULTANT
Leah Culver

PHOTOGRAPHS ©: cover: lassedesignen/Shutterstock, Inc.; 3: Monkey Business Images/Shutterstock, Inc.; 4 left: Volker Steger/Science Source; 4 right: Rick Scibelli, Jr./AP Images; 5 left: kupicoo/iStockphoto; 5 right: epa european pressphoto agency b.v./Alamy Images; 6: funstock/iStockphoto; 8: Pictorial Press Ltd/Alamy Images; 9: Mark Dunn/Alamy images; 10 top: SWNS; 10 bottom: Apic/Getty Images; 11 top: Volker Steger/Science Source; 11 bottom: Geoffrey Biddle/Getty Images; 12: Alfred Eisenstaedt/Getty Images; 13: Bettmann/Corbis Images; 14: Interfoto/Alamy Images; 15: David Cooper/Getty Images; 16: AP Images; 17: Keith Beaty/Getty Images; 18: Jim Spelios Feature Photo Service/Newscom; 19: Gary Burchell/Getty Images; 20: TommL/iStockphoto; 22: Thomas Barwick/Getty Images; 23: Rick Scibelli, Jr./AP Images; 24 left: dpa picture alliance archive/Alamy Images; 24 right-25 left, 25 right: epa european pressphoto agency b.v./Alamy Images; 26, 27: Monkey Business Images/Shutterstock, Inc.; 28, 29 top: Fred Prouser/Landov; 29 bottom: Hank Morgan/Shutterstock, Inc.; 30: Victor J. Blue/Bloomberg via Getty Images; 31: Monkey Business Images/Shutterstock, Inc.; 32: skynesher/iStockphoto; 34: TommL/iStockphoto; 35: Dragon Images/Shutterstock, Inc.; 36 left: Børth Aadne Sætrenes/Getty Images; 36 right: Flirt/Alamy Images; 37: GDA via AP Images; 38: kupicoo/iStockphoto; 39: Goodluz/Shutterstock, Inc.; 40: Leah Culver; 42: alvarez/iStockphoto; 43: Andrew Holbrooke/Corbis Images; 44: epa european pressphoto agency b.v./Alamy Images; 46: Leonardo Patrizi/iStockphoto; 47: Cian O'Day; 48: Aerial Archives/Alamy Images; 49: View Pictures Ltd/Alamy Images; 50: Microsoft News Center; 51: Darkworx/Dreamstime; 52: rawcaptured/Shutterstock, Inc.; 53 top: Microsoft News Center; 53 bottom: Joseph Branston/Linux Format Magazine via Getty Images; 54: sturti/iStockphoto; 55: Bill Hinton/Getty Images; 56: Hasloo/iStockphoto; 57: Melanie Stetson Freeman/The Christian Science Monitor via Getty Images; 58 bottom: PC Garner Magazine/Getty Images; 58 top: Kin Cheung/AP Images; 59: Junko Kimura/Bloomberg via Getty Image.

LIBRARY OF CONGRESS CATALOGING-IN-PUBLICATION DATA
Mara, Wil, author.
 Software development : science, technology, and engineering / by Wil Mara.
   pages cm. — (Calling all innovators : a career for you)
 Summary: "Learn about the history of software development and find out what it takes to make it in this exciting career field."— Provided by publisher.
 ISBN 978-0-531-23003-9 (library binding : alk. paper) — ISBN 978-0-531-23221-7 (pbk. : alk. paper)
 1. Computer software—Development—Juvenile literature. 2. Computer programming—Vocational guidance—Juvenile literature. I. Title. II. Series: Calling all innovators.
 QA76.76.D47M3615 2016
 005.1—dc23                                   2015032936

All rights reserved. Published in 2016 by Children's Press, an imprint of Scholastic Inc.
Printed in the United States of America 113

1 2 3 4 5 6 7 8 9 10 R 25 24 23 22 21 20 19 18 17 16

# CALLING ALL  INNOVATORS

## A CAREER FOR YOU

Science, technology, engineering, the arts, and math are the fields that drive innovation. Whether they are finding ways to make our lives easier or developing the latest entertainment, the people who work in these fields are changing the world for the better. Do you have what it takes to join the ranks of today's greatest innovators? Read on to discover if a career in the exciting world of software development is for you.

# TABLE *of* CONTENTS

Computer hardware has gotten much smaller and more powerful over time.

Many of today's developers focus on creating software for tablet computers.

*Creating software involves close collaboration among team members.*

*Microsoft's Windows 10 operating system took years to develop.*

The range of devices that rely on software is constantly growing and changing.

1

# THE NONHUMAN TOUCH

Some people may believe the world is still in the earliest stages of the computer age. In truth, humankind has been trying for hundreds of years to build a machine that "thinks." Many people have wanted something that can make their lives a bit more efficient. Let's face it—writing a book report is much easier to do using Microsoft Word than a typewriter. And staying in touch with your friends is much quicker through texting or Facebook than snail mail. Computers have changed the way we do just about everything these days, but without the right **software**, they'd be about as useful as a flat tire.

## MILESTONES IN PROGRAMMING

| 1840s | 1957 | 1970 | 1972 | 1983 |
|---|---|---|---|---|
| Ada Lovelace writes programs for Charles Babbage's Analytical Engine. | IBM develops the FORTRAN programming language. | The PASCAL programming language is introduced, for use in both commercial and scientific applications. | The C programming language is released. | Microsoft launches its word-processing program called Word. |

*Ada Lovelace was encouraged by her mother to study math.*

# THE FIRST PROGRAMMER

Many experts consider Ada King, Countess of Lovelace, the first person to have attempted writing software, in the early 1800s. Lovelace is now more often known simply as Ada Lovelace. A talented mathematician, Lovelace was a good friend of Charles Babbage. Babbage had a range of interests, from mathematics and engineering to writing and philosophy. He was also an inventor.

## ADA LOVELACE

Math and science were widely considered unsuitable for women in 19th century Britain. Ada Lovelace was one remarkable exception. Lovelace was the daughter of Annabella Milbanke Byron and the poet George Gordon Byron, 6th Baron Byron, popularly known as Lord Byron. The Byrons' marriage was not an easy one. Within months of Ada's birth, her parents separated and her father permanently left the country.

Lord Byron was famous for his difficult and flamboyant personality. Lady Byron wanted desperately to separate her daughter from that life. She hired private tutors in math, science, music, and languages in an effort to do so. Ada was naturally clever and curious. She eventually married William King, Earl of Lovelace, and used her wealth, social connections, and intelligence to continue her studies.

One of Babbage's most important creations was the design of a machine he called an Analytical Engine. He hoped this device would be the first computing machine to perform complex arithmetic. It was pretty advanced for its time. It could store information and perform an **algorithm**, or set of step-by-step instructions. As Babbage worked on his design, Lovelace created an algorithm for it. Unfortunately, his computer was never completed and the algorithm never put to use. Nevertheless, Lovelace wrote herself into history as the very first computer programmer.

# TURING'S MACHINE

Another legendary English mathematician took the next big steps in software engineering. Alan Turing had long been interested in computing machines. In 1937, he published a paper theorizing that such a machine could perform a range of complex operations. It just needed specific and accurate algorithms to tell it what to do. The device became known as the Turing Machine. Some experts today consider this the basis of all modern computers and their programs.

During World War II (1939–1945), Turing developed code-breaking machines. These devices were extremely complex but designed to execute only a single algorithm. After the war ended, Turing returned to the idea of programming a computer to do multiple tasks. He described a computer able to store its own programs electronically within its memory. This was known as ACE—the Automatic Computing Engine. Turing moved on to other pursuits a short time later without building a model of the device. However, he did produce a paper in 1948 that further detailed his thoughts on a software-driven computer. It was not published until after his death in June 1954. But the paper and his machine are now considered benchmarks in the development of computer programming.

*The first version of Turing's Automatic Computing Engine, Pilot ACE, ran its first program in 1950.*

9

# FIRST THINGS FIRST

*Ralph Benjamin was not able to share his roller ball technology with the public for many years.*

## MAKING MICE

These days, you can usually scroll, click, shrink, and even type with the touch of a finger. But touch screens weren't always what we used to navigate programs. Before them, there was the mouse.

## A MILITARY SECRET

The year was 1946. British naval scientist Ralph Benjamin was working on a program to predict the paths of enemy planes. The program plotted plane positions on a grid. It used data that a person entered via an input device. Benjamin tried a number of different input devices, including a joystick. But what worked best was a new invention he called a roller ball. This was a metal ball guided by two small, rubber-coated wheels. However, the public didn't hear about the roller ball for many decades. As a military tool, it was kept secret. A similar device was created with the Royal Canadian Navy. It, too, was kept from the public.

## A WOODEN BOX

In the mid-1960s, American inventor Douglas Engelbart came up with something much closer to the computer mouse we use today. It was a small, brown box of polished wood with a narrow cable running from one end. The design looked a bit like a mouse, which earned the device its name. The mouse had two wheels underneath running perpendicular to each other. There was also a tiny red button on top of the box, tucked in one corner.

*Douglas Englebart's device may look basic compared to more recent mice, but it was revolutionary for its time.*

**BUTTON**

**CABLE CONNECTS TO COMPUTER**

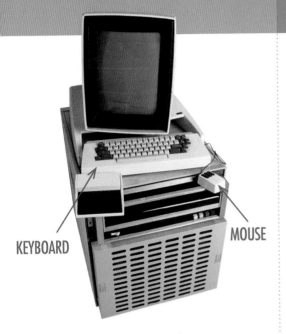

KEYBOARD     MOUSE

*The Xerox Alto system came with a monitor, keyboard, and mouse.*

## PUBLIC APPEARANCE

Mouse technology continued to improve steadily over the years. The first computers to include a mouse began shipping in the 1970s. In 1973, Xerox introduced the Alto, one of the very first personal computers available to the general public. The computer was in a horizontal case with a keyboard and a **monitor**. A mouse attached to it by a wire. A person could use both the keyboard and the mouse to control operations on the computer. This made the Alto highly advanced for its time. Unfortunately, the Alto was so expensive that very few users could afford one.

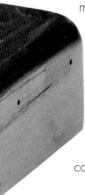

## MODERN MOUSE

Bill Gates, founder of the software company Microsoft, saw the mouse's potential. It made computers easier to use, and that would encourage more people to buy computers and software. With this in mind, Microsoft started making its products more mouse-friendly in the early 1980s. The company also developed its own mouse in 1983. Later that same year, Apple introduced the Lisa mouse, which was included in its Apple Lisa computer system.

*Many of Microsoft's programs are built so people can navigate them easily with a mouse.*

## THE BINARY METHOD

Binary **code** is one method of telling computers what to do. You may have seen this code represented as a series of *1*s and *0*s. Each number represents one bit, or binary digit. A bit is a computer's most basic unit of information. When strung together in certain patterns, several bits equal one instruction. American mathematician and engineer Claude Shannon was heavily involved in developing the binary system of programming. Shannon produced a paper on its value called "A Mathematical Theory of Communication," published in *The Bell System Technical Journal* in 1948.

Computer programmers began embracing the binary system despite the fact that it was remarkably tedious. Inputting binary code

could require anything from feeding hole-punched cards through the machine to plugging wires in and unplugging wires from a **circuit** board. There was no room for error, either—one mistake and the entire program would be derailed. This usually required the programmer to start over from scratch. Most computer systems at the time were built for governments, businesses, schools, and similar institutions. Binary programs were custom designed for each institution's needs.

*American engineer Claude Shannon was one of the first people to use the word "bit."*

*The U.S. Census Bureau began using computers in the 1950s.*

# WATCHING THEIR LANGUAGE

By the 1950s, computers were used in many businesses and organizations. New computers continued to be built, with customers requesting more specific design requirements. This meant that most new computers were built from the ground up. While they were based on existing computers with similar functions, most new systems needed customized **hardware** and software for their particular purpose. It was not unusual for programmers to create entirely new programs for every customer. As systems became more advanced and more common, requests poured in for new computers.

Programmers needed to keep up with this demand, but binary code was extremely time-consuming. To solve the issue, programmers created programming **languages**. These used words or phrases to create common computer instructions. For example, *and* or + might indicate addition. *For each* followed by *in* could represent checking items off a list. The new languages made it simpler to turn out new programs. This was an important step in the evolution of software development. Programming languages proved extremely successful, and they are standard tools for developers today.

## SIMPLIFYING THINGS

You may have heard the acronym *GUI* (often pronounced "gooey") in relation to computers. It stands for "graphical user **interface**." This is a fancy phrase for a program that makes it easy for a person to work with a computer system. A computer functions through line **commands**, coding, algorithms, and so on. These can be baffling for the average user. The GUI acts as an easily understood and attractive go-between. For example, instead of typing out commands to open a Web browser, a person simply moves the **cursor** on the screen and clicks on the browser's icon, or symbol.

## DIGITAL DESK

Apple introduced one of the first important GUIs for home computers in 1983. It was programmed into a computer known as the Lisa. The Lisa's GUI had revolutionary new features. One of the most striking was the multipanel window feature. A user could have several programs open in separate "windows" at

one time. This allowed the user to work on multiple tasks more easily and efficiently.

The Lisa's GUI also emphasized a desktop-like appearance, re-creating on-screen the feel of looking down at one's desk. For example, an open document appeared as a piece of paper. Other elements included a calculator, a notepad, and a clock.

*A program opened as a window on the Lisa's screen.*

**BUILT-IN MONITOR**

A demonstrator shows how Microsoft's Windows 1.0 software works on a computer in 1986.

DISK DRIVE

## CONTINUING INNOVATION

By 1986, Apple was shipping out units with a full-color GUI. You could even customize it, although choices were limited. Microsoft successfully produced its own **operating system** in 1985. It was called Windows 1.0 and worked similarly to Apple's system. ✳

*Employees at the California Department of Motor Vehicles feed data into the department's computers in 1969.*

## DEMAND EXCEEDS SUPPLY

As the popularity of industrial computers began its epic rise, there followed a need for more software. Unfortunately, there was not enough software to satisfy that need, nor were there enough programmers to address the need efficiently. A "software crisis" period occurred for much of the 1960s through the 1980s. Just about every aspect of software development teetered on the brink of catastrophe. Customers—still almost exclusively businesses, schools, and other organizations—were making increasingly complicated demands of software developers. Those developers were often bewildered as to how to best create the software.

With such a high demand, new programs were often built as quickly as possible. Many of these programs are considered standard today, such as spreadsheet programs like the modern Excel. But computer hardware was growing more powerful, too, and software companies did not yet understand how to take advantage of it. There was no standard code language to make it easier to move from one program to the next. Thus, countless projects ran way over budget, sailed past deadlines, and failed to meet customer requirements. They were also unreliable and unstable in their coding. This made it almost impossible to create improved versions of existing software.

# GETTING THEIR ACT TOGETHER

In response to the software crisis, programmers began discussing ways to refine the development process. One of the most important issues was standardizing the way a new program was created. In order to create good programs efficiently, their development had to be fairly organized. Haphazard or disorganized work methods were often unreliable, with unpredictable results. In response, developers worked on general steps for people to follow along a sensible timeline. For example, a developer first determined the requirements of the program. Then he or she built it, tested it, installed it, and finally maintained it. All the while, programmers would study ways to improve the software for next time.

Back then, the average software developer did not have all the tools that are available today. Government standards, maintenance systems, peer review and feedback, and numerous other tools arose from the need for a more efficient and reliable developmental process.

*A programmer tests a new computer graphic system in 1986.*

# GROWING AND CHANGING

When the Internet became available to the public in the late 20th century, it provided developers incredible opportunities. They could communicate with one another, compare notes, and test and design new software like never before. It was also around this time that home computers became common. Ordinary people needed software to address a range of needs, from e-mail to home finance to word processing. As a result, the software market took off like a rocket.

As more people went online, software developers had to make it easier to use and navigate the Web. This gave rise to Web browsers and new languages, such as HTML, made just for the Internet. Over time, designers began adding photos, videos, links between sites, interactive tools, search engines, and databases. This provided Internet users with a richer experience. At the same time, software developers met the challenge of online crime by creating special protective programs.

More recently, a new market emerged with the introduction of smartphones, tablets, and other mobile devices. This led to a new boom in software development: mobile apps. From video games to business meetings, almost anything can now be done on mobile devices. Programmers make each and every one of those activities possible. These days, almost anyone in software development has worked in the mobile market at some point.

*Developers worked on a huge range of new Web sites in the 1990s. Internet sites now do everything from providing entertainment to assessing cancer risk.*

*Software developers constantly work to understand customers' demands and how to meet them.*

## TODAY

Software development has gone through many much-needed refinements. And it is still evolving. In fact, anyone involved in software development knows that it will never be settled or finished. It is always growing, always changing. Today, developers are keyed in to ideas that suit the fast-moving world in which we live. Modern development methods place an emphasis on speed, usability, and timely delivery. Many of these methods have a stripped-down approach to creating programs. Others are more work-intensive. Some methods rely on cooperation, not just within one development team, but also among several separate teams. Open-source software functions this way. Open-source products are freely available to anyone who wants to use them. Free, ready-to-use code has made software development faster than ever.

This ever-shifting field may be challenging. However, those who can adapt to and meet those challenges can look forward to a fair degree of job security and relatively high pay.

Many developers work long hours to make sure programs are completed on time.

# CHAPTER TWO

# SO MANY OPTIONS

**D**esigning software is a complicated process. Developers need to have intense focus and exceptional attention to detail. For some people, a job in this field may also require a lot of long hours. On the upside, there is a wide range of ways to create something in the world of technology. Some methods focus on speed, while others try to minimize risk as much as possible. There are methods that begin with a stripped-down version of the product and methods that deliver a product in bits and pieces. Some of the most common approaches to software development are presented here.

## THE POSSIBLE FUTURE OF TECHNOLOGY

| 2017 | 2020 | 2025 | 2035 |
|------|------|------|------|
| Microchips less than 10 nanometers in size are common. (For comparison, a strand of human DNA is only about 2.5 nm in diameter.) | Most of Earth's population of more than seven billion people have access to the Internet. | All cell phone users will be able to see each other in three-dimensional holographic images. | Designers develop the first computers with true artificial intelligence. |

*The waterfall model requires extensive preplanning.*

## THE WATERFALL MODEL

One of the most common methods of software development is the waterfall model. This approach largely consists of matching the needs to existing hardware. The first step, therefore, is critical: determining what the software needs to do and how it needs to do it. This is when a developer must accurately assess a client's needs. Mistakes will be extremely difficult (and expensive) to correct later on. The developers often work with the customers directly. Together, they can determine what the final product should be.

Next comes analysis. This is a sort of gaming phase. The early ideas are tried out using models and similar preliminary methods. Then the architects design the software, and the coders begin to build it. The next step, testing, is essential. Programmers know that it's better to comb out all bugs, or problems, long before the software is officially put to use. In some instances, testing is done on-site with the customer, creating as close to real-life situations as possible. Finally, there is the operability phase. At this point, the customer officially starts using the software as the developers provide support, fixing any bugs or issues that come up.

# NOTHING BUT A SKELETON

The prototyping method has been around for decades. A prototype is the earliest version of something. Where software is concerned, a developer puts together an early and very simple version of a program. This preliminary version is not necessarily "pretty." In other words, it doesn't possess all the streamlined interfacing that the finished product will have. It may also lack some extra features that will be added later on. The idea is to present a stripped-down version of the program so it can be tested before further development. The features included in a prototype are usually those that will be used most often in the finished product. Often, the prototype is given to multiple users to try. Then a programmer gets their feedback and makes notes on where to improve.

Prototyping can take a lot of time to perform, but it is a great tool if a project's deadline allows it. In fact, it is not unusual for a project schedule to have multiple "milestone deadlines" before the final deadline. In these cases, developers produce a prototype very early in the process and then adjust it as needed. It is also common for a final product to end up being very different from the initial prototype.

*A programmer tests a new program on a tablet computer.*

*Blue Gene computers are very large, with multiple sections.*

## NOW *THAT'S* A SUPERCOMPUTER

Blue Gene is one of the most powerful supercomputers of all time. Actually, there are several different supercomputers that bear the Blue Gene label. A company called IBM designed them all with the aim of being remarkably fast while consuming very little power. Thanks to lightning-fast processing speeds, Blue Gene computers have been used for some impressive applications.

## MAPPING THE BRAIN

One of the most interesting uses for Blue Gene was an attempt to copy the form and function of the human brain. The human brain is extremely complex. Billions of neurons process, store, and distribute all the information that passes through it. Even the Blue Gene system couldn't cover this completely. However, programmers were able to design software that successfully simulated about 4.5 percent of the average brain.

# PLAYING GAMES

In 2010, Veselin Topalov used a Blue Gene system to prepare for that year's word chess championship. In 1997, chess master Garry Kasparov played a match against an earlier supercomputer called Deep Blue. It was created by the same company that later designed Blue Gene. Though Kasparov had beaten similar computers

*Blue Gene's thousands of computer chips and connectors process vast amounts of information.*

*Veselin Topalov (above) and other chess masters use advanced computer systems to prepare for matches.*

before, this time he lost. With this in mind, Topalov considered a supercomputer an excellent opponent to help him practice. However, no chess software existed for Blue Gene at the time. To solve this issue, programmers adapted chess programs that had been designed for other systems. ✳

# AROUND AND AROUND WE GO

The agile method of software development is perhaps one of the most interesting. It focuses heavily on adaptability and fast, continuous development. First, developers try to predict as many of a program's requirements and potential issues as possible. Then they go through multiple rounds of product development, weeding out any bugs as they go. Each round builds upon the one before it. As the software evolves, developers adopt elements of one or more other methods, such as waterfall or prototyping.

A key feature in the agile approach is to focus on a different aspect of the program with each pass of the cycle. Developers inspect and test a program from a variety of approaches. Over time, each aspect is refined and tightened. In a way, the agile approach is the ultimate form of development modeling. Every facet of a program is given close attention long before delivery of the final product.

*Developers working as a team often need to talk through problems to find the best solution.*

*Customers can start putting incremental software to use almost immediately.*

## PIECE BY PIECE

In many cases, developers deliver new software to the customers as one complete package. In the incremental approach, it is designed one piece, or increment, at a time. Each piece is then passed to the customer for evaluation. Only after all the pieces are delivered will the customer have a complete product. This approach allows both the customer and the development team to solve problems long before the finished program is in place. Similarly, none of the changes made during each phase are likely to be overwhelming, as the problems are instead being addressed in small bits at a time. Another advantage is that the customer can start using the program without having to wait for the whole thing to be finished. This is similar in some ways to the spiral method. A customer can dictate which software elements are most important, and programmers develop those first.

There are disadvantages to the incremental method as well. For one, the overall final cost of the software may exceed initial expectations. This is particularly true if numerous and extensive changes are needed at each stage. Also, this approach does not account for problems that occur when all elements of a program are pieced together.

# FROM THIS TO THAT

*The team working on ARPANET at UCLA used this processor, called an Interface Message Processor.*

## BUILDING A NETWORK

Can you guess when the Internet was first created? The 1990s? Late 1980s? Try earlier. The World Wide Web as we know it today started as a very small, very quiet experiment in the late 1960s.

## THE ARPANET?

In 1969, the U.S. Department of Defense's Advanced Research Projects Agency (ARPA) wanted to try building a digital network that connected computers. The computers would be located at the University of California, Los Angeles (UCLA), University of California, Santa Barbara (UCSB), Stanford University (which is in California), and the University of Utah. The developers working on the project called the network ARPANET, and they soon met with success. The first message made it through the network on the evening of October 29, 1969.

ARPANET quickly grew as other facilities signed up. In 1973, the system went international when a facility in Norway joined. That same year, developers began work on TCP/IP (Transmission Control **Protocol**/Internet

29OCT69 2100 LOADED OP. PROGRAM (S)
FOR BEN BARKER
BBN

22:30 Talked to SRI
Host to Host CS(C

Left op. imp program CS(C
running after sending
a host dead message
to imp.

30 Oct69 1030 Stopped op. prog

*A note in the official logbook from 1969 shows the contents of the first e-mail ever sent.*

Protocol). This protocol now forms the backbone of how computers communicate with one another through the Internet. E-mail—and the programs that make it easy to use—was also becoming more common.

## WORLD WIDE WEB

Dial-up connections, which used phone lines to connect computers to the Internet, became openly available to everyday users in 1989. Around the same time, Tim Berners-Lee of the European Organization for Nuclear Research (CERN) changed the Internet forever. How? He designed a new approach to distributing information around the Internet. He called it the World Wide Web. Users could navigate it through an attractive GUI and access any online "documents." By the mid-1990s, developers released applications known as browsers to make Web viewing and navigation even easier. By 2015, there were nearly 1 billion Web sites worldwide. ✳

*Tim Berners-Lee became famous as the creator of the World Wide Web.*

*One mistake in coding can cause many unexpected problems.*

## UNTIL YOU GET IT RIGHT

The iterative development process is, to many, the most intuitive method for designing software. In simplest terms, it means to design a program in its entirety, put it through thorough testing, then go back and fix any problems that turned up. This approach assumes there will be flaws and challenges right from the start. Developers using the iterative process hope that the majority of problems will be identified in the earliest stages of testing. As a result, each successive stage would pose fewer difficulties until the program is ready for release.

The word *iteration* fits the process well. It means a version or form of something. In some cases, a team of programmers will personally work with each version of the program themselves. Other times, they will have outsiders test the software and provide as much feedback as possible. It is unusual, however, for iterative development to involve giving the software over to customers for live evaluation, as in the incremental process.

# HURRY UP!

A developmental method that has picked up in popularity in recent years is known as rapid development. As its name suggests, the focus is on speed. That means certain steps are either shortened or eliminated. The initial planning and design stages, for example, are almost nonexistent.

The process often starts with a customer, such as a business, providing a list of requirements that a new program needs to fill. The developer may then work directly with the client to code and build the program as quickly as possible. Program testing begins almost immediately. Testing is done using an iterative method. Programmers fix bugs and make improvements, refining the program in one version after another until it is fully functional. Many of the fancier features common in other programs may be left behind in rapid development. For example, the user interface might not be as attractive as in programs that spent a longer time in development.

As with all software, a rapidly developed program will be judged by its ability to perform its assigned function. The key advantage to the rapid method is cost. Because it requires much less time and usually fewer programmers, the development is much less expensive than with other methods.

*Rapid software developers focus more on a program's functionality and less on its appearance.*

Computer science students will likely spend a lot of time in class at computer labs during college.

# CHAPTER THREE

# ON THE JOB

The software development field has seen significant growth in the past few decades. This is likely to continue in the years ahead. Those who are interested in a career in this field should focus on areas of study such as computer programming and technology, electronics, mathematics, and similar areas. A college education is required in virtually all areas. The pay is also quite good, as this is a high-interest discipline with a broad and bright future.

## NOTABLE SOFTWARE SETBACKS

| 1983 | 1987 | 1997 | 1999 | 2003 |
| --- | --- | --- | --- | --- |
| An attack-detection system in the USSR (now Russia) misinterprets the movement of the sun's reflection on clouds as five launched missiles. | A programming error causes a cancer treatment machine to deliver dangerously high doses of radiation. | The USS Yorktown's propulsion system loses all power when a crew member accidentally misfeeds a command into the ship's software. | Developers frantically update computer systems and software to prevent glitches when switching from 1999, often entered as 99, to 2000, or 00. | A power plant along Lake Erie shuts down in part because software fails to alert engineers of developing issues. |

## THE ENGINEER

A software engineer is involved in the nuts-and-bolts production of software. He or she can take part in virtually any aspect of software development—brainstorming, creation, testing, maintenance, and so on. The better engineers are familiar with all these steps and all disciplines related to the field. Engineers can sit for long hours at a desk and write line after line of code. Or they can go on-site with a customer and observe how a program they've already written is doing.

An engineering position has tremendous flexibility. Engineers can work on a job site, in an office, or from home—or any combination of these. They can be full-time or part-time employees. An engineer could even be an outside **vendor** who owns a small company. The average engineer works about 40 hours a week, which is standard for most jobs. However, when a project is nearing completion, an engineer could work 60 or 70 hours in a week. Engineers are expected to keep up on all the latest technology. They must also be able to work both in a group environment and on their own.

*Software engineers at some companies can choose when and where to do their work.*

*A QA tester frequently takes extensive notes on issues found during testing.*

## OPTIMIZERS AND QA WORKERS

Performance **optimization** might not be the most glamorous profession in the tech universe. However, it's certainly one of the most important. An optimizer's job is to push every piece of new software to its limits. Optimizers are involved in nearly every stage of development. They work with engineers, marketing people, and the software's users. Optimizers make sure the software performs correctly with the hardware, other programs, and other elements that will be present when the software is used. Then they provide feedback to engineers to fix any issues. Optimizers may also come up with their own ideas for improving the next version of a program. Innovative, outside-the-box thinking is often a valuable trait in this position.

A quality assurance (QA) person is similar to an optimizer. The difference is that a QA worker focuses more on a product at the end of its development. These experts test every conceivable aspect of the program, from graphics and interaction to Internet and hardware compatibility. Some QA people design their own tests. Others follow a set of tasks provided by the manufacturer. Even one failure means the software goes back to the developers. QA work can be fun, but it also requires considerable expertise and experience.

*A GUI like the one on Apple's iPad may take years to develop.*

How a piece of software should look and feel to a user informs much of a program's design. Using line commands, coding, or algorithms to navigate is not easy. Nor is it particularly eye-catching. A prettier, easier-to-use GUI solves this problem. And the programmers who design these GUIs tap into the artistic side of software design.

## MAKING IT BIG

GUI design became a major part of creating software in the 1980s. Home computer sales were beginning to soar. Computers and software started being marketed more for the average user. Hardware companies realized that one way they could increase sales was by making their products better looking than their competitors'.

Apple quickly became one of the leaders in the field during this decade. The company paid close attention to the pleasing visual aspects of its operating system. Microsoft made its own move in this direction in 1995 with Windows 95. In terms of artistry, it was an improvement over from the operating system before it. Windows 95 has even been the basis for all Windows GUIs since then. Today, the

*Windows 95's colorful GUI helped make it a huge success.*

*This Google doodle celebrates the life of Italian composer Giovacchino Antonio Rossini.*

average user has a choice of colorful and easy interfaces at their command. These systems are also more customizable than ever before.

## ART IN ADVERTISING

Having a good GUI is only one part of program artistry. A company also has to convince people to use it. The people the company hires to do this have to understand and believe in the product. Advertising can take the form of posters, billboards, big presentation events, or commercials. Google uses what they call "doodles." Google doodlers make changes to the company's logo on the Google homepage. The doodles celebrate famous birthdays, holidays, important moments in history, and other events.

They might be simple drawings, short animations, or even interactive games. Whatever form they take, the doodles attract users to their site, encouraging more people to use their services.

Google created its first doodle in 1998, not long after the company was founded. But doodling really started to take off in 2000 with a highly successful illustration celebrating France's Bastille Day. Since then, an elite team of doodlers has created thousands of illustrations for the Web site. Some doodles appear only for people in a certain country or region. Others can be viewed around the world. Entertained users can share the doodles on Facebook, Twitter, and other social media. This gains Google even more attention. ☀

*A software architect must be a leader, keeping people on track and letting them know what to do.*

# THE SOFTWARE ARCHITECT

Some people are big-picture thinkers. Others are better at thinking about the details. Then there are those who are good at both. Software architects usually fall into this last category. A software architect helps develop new programs on all levels, from the original big idea to the tiniest final features.

In many cases, a project really begins with the software architect. This is the person who identifies a client's or the public's latest software demands. He or she then creates the blueprint that everyone else on the development team will follow. Architects have to always keep the general progress and goals of a project in mind. This helps them understand how everything will fit together and keep the project on track. Members of a development team may focus on particular parts of a project. But architects have to focus on all the parts. They are responsible for defining each aspect of a project. This is one of the most critical, challenging, and rewarding jobs in software development, requiring a broad field of knowledge.

# THE SYSTEM ARCHITECT

A system architect is similar to a software architect in that he or she thinks big and oversees an entire project. For a system architect, however, there is less focus on the programs within a system and more focus on the system itself. A system is an existing structure within which software runs and hardware functions. Think of it like a Christmas tree: A computer's programs and hardware are the decorations that hang on it. The system is the tree itself.

The system architect ensures a system is friendly not just to the user but to all the parts that run within it. Different software must be able to work together when necessary and not get in the way otherwise. All hardware also needs to function exactly as designed with the system.

The system architect works with other developers on many different levels to assure full harmony between software, hardware, and system. The architect must also foresee with reasonable accuracy any upcoming problems. This job requires an awareness of the latest technologies and the intellect to understand their implications.

*A system architect helps make sure a program will work on a desktop computer, a tablet, and other types of hardware.*

*Leah Culver is a developer advocate (someone who supports a company's developers) at Dropbox. She is also an iPhone app developer.*

**When did you start thinking about getting into the field of computer programming? What was it about this discipline that interested/inspired you?** I started thinking about becoming a computer programmer when I was in college. I was studying graphic design and took a programming class as part of my studies and really loved it. I've always enjoyed solving puzzles, and programming is a lot like solving puzzles in order to create something new, which is exactly what I love doing.

**What kinds of classes did you take in middle school, high school, and beyond in order to prepare for your career?** I wasn't aware of any computer programming classes in middle or high school, although I did teach myself how to make Web pages using HTML in high school. My friends and I would make Web pages about ourselves and share them with each other. In college, I studied computer science and really enjoyed all my programming classes, especially the ones in Web programming.

**What other projects and jobs did you do in school and your work life before beginning your career? And how did that work prepare you?** The most important thing I did to learn computer programming was to practice a lot. I liked to build simple computer games to teach myself new skills. I built a minesweeper game in Java, a brick-breaker game in Flash, and a solitaire game in JavaScript. I had so much fun building games! Throughout high school and college, I worked various jobs including being a cashier at a grocery store and a hostess at a restaurant. I learned how to show up on time, get my work done, and work with other people—all important skills to have for any job.

**Do you have a particular project that you're especially proud of or that you think really took your work to another level?** The first Web application I built from scratch really took my skills to the next level. I learned everything from how to set up a database and Web server to how to correctly write HTML and CSS. It was a huge project, and I was so proud to have finished it. I'm also really proud of the first mobile app I built. Mobile programming is very different from Web programming, so I was excited to be able to learn something completely new.

**It obviously takes teamwork to make things happen in the field of computer programming. Does working as part of a team come naturally to you, or was it something you had to learn and work on?** I really enjoy working on teams with other enthusiastic engineers. It's fun to build something together that I couldn't build on my own. I like getting feedback from others and working together to solve big problems. I started out writing most of my programs by myself with help from friends and other students, which was a good way to learn. However, I think it's much more interesting to work with other people.

**What would your dream project be if you were given unlimited resources?** My dream project is always changing, and I've been lucky to be able to build a lot of the things I've wanted to. My current dream project is to help users be safer and more secure online. I'd like to explore different ways for people to log on to Web sites and mobile apps and make the experience both more secure and easier to do.

**What advice would you give to a young person who wants to do what you do one day?** Go for it! Computer programming is a very fun and challenging field where you can learn new things every day. I'm never bored! I love being able to dream up an app and build it. It's a very creative job, and I never stop making new things. ☀

# THE TECHNICAL CONSULTANT

A technical consultant often serves as both the face of a company and the voice of the customers who the company serves. A consultant has a broad knowledge of every aspect of software creation. He or she is particularly knowledgeable about how a piece of software is meant to function.

Consultants are essentially a bridge between the company and the customer. They work with customers to ensure software does what it is required to do. Good consultants know how to observe and listen. They can put themselves in a customer's head and see things from that person's perspective. Consultants know how to separate unimportant details from those that are critical. They then present that important information to the development teams in a way that is clear and precise. Consultants should also be able to get a sense of what new needs the software must fulfill in the future. Often, technical consultants may have to predict potential problems *before* they arise. For example, they might work with program features that seem perfectly fine to a user but may cause trouble down the road.

Technical consultants make sure developers understand what customers need or what problems a customer faces with a program.

*A good catchphrase accurately describes a product and is appealing to potential customers. Android's motto, "be together, not the same," highlights the system's customizability.*

## THE MARKETING ENGINEER

People who have a broad knowledge of software design and are good at connecting with people are ideal marketing engineers. These engineers are in charge of spreading the word about a project and inspiring customers to purchase it. This is not just a matter of smart salesmanship. The job also requires a deep knowledge of the specific software and how it can be most valuable to a user.

Marketing engineers often begin by analyzing data on the types of programs people are buying. This helps them to understand a customer's needs now and to predict what those needs may be in the future. Engineers then pass that information to the program's designers. When a product is nearly ready for release, marketing engineers come up with new and interesting ways to advertise it. They help create demonstrations, study competing products, and work on distribution and ad campaigns. They also provide ongoing support throughout the advertising process.

This is a crucial position in today's tech industry. Even the best software in the world won't have much success if customers don't know it exists!

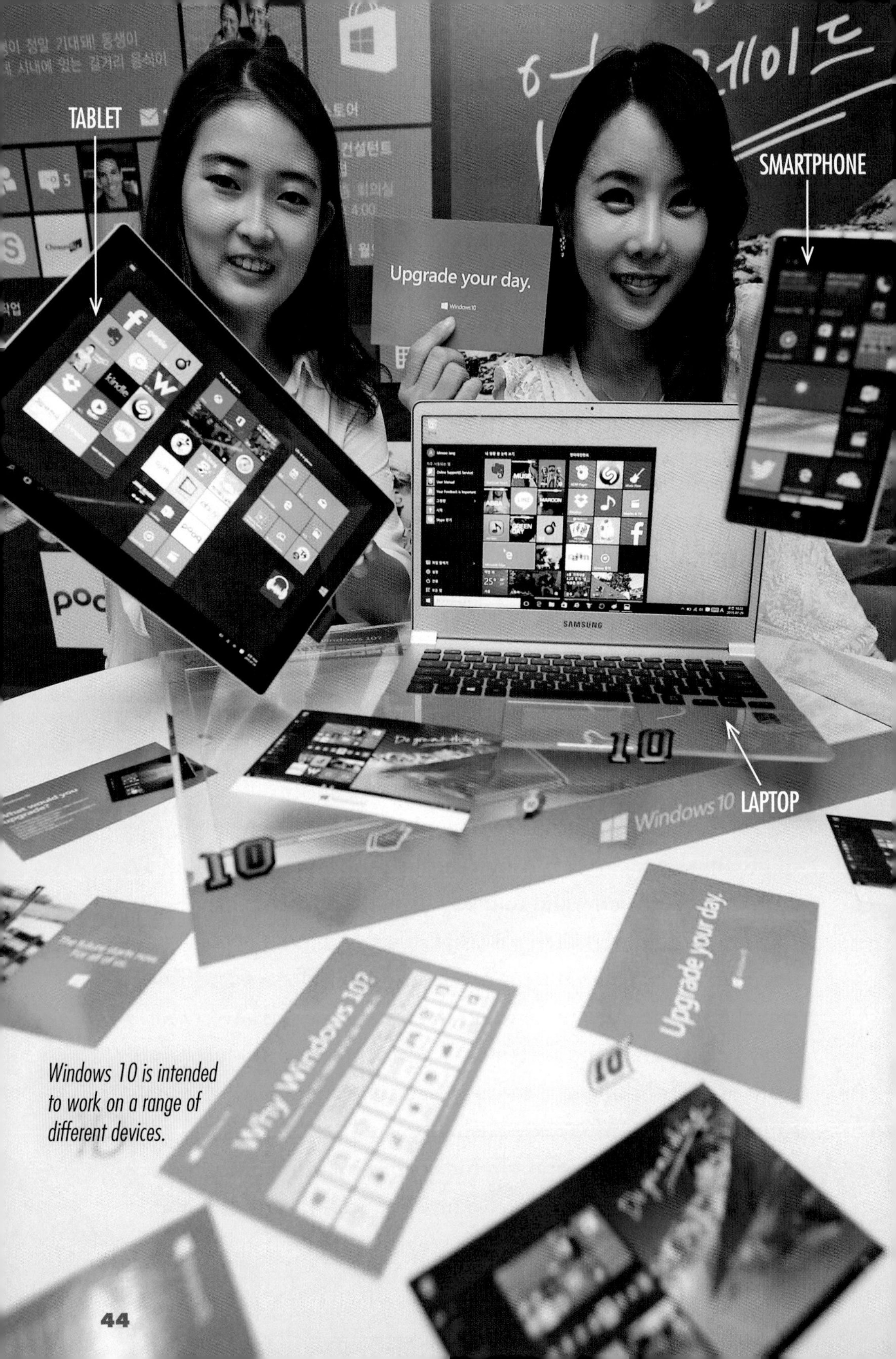

TABLET
SMARTPHONE
LAPTOP
Upgrade your day.
Windows 10
SAMSUNG
Windows 10
Why Windows 10?
Upgrade your day.

*Windows 10 is intended to work on a range of different devices.*

4

# BUILDING THE PERFECT BEAST

D eveloping computer software is like creating anything else: it goes one step at a time. In the chapter ahead, we'll look at this from both a general perspective and through the example of Microsoft's Windows 10 operating system, released in 2015. As programs become increasingly complex, so does the process of making them. Yes, the process has become streamlined in many ways. But public demand for bigger and better programs is also increasing, and it can be challenging to keep up with that. On the upside, however, each new major software project represents some small advancement in knowledge and experience.

## A BRIEF HISTORY OF MICROSOFT WINDOWS

| 1985 | 1995 | 2001 | 2012 | 2015 |
|------|------|------|------|------|
| Microsoft releases its first operating system, Windows 1.0. | Windows 95 is released, selling seven million copies in five weeks. | Microsoft releases Windows XP, a heavily redesigned version of its operating system. | Windows 8 debuts with a redesign that features tiles and apps. | Microsoft releases Windows 10. |

*Developers need to be aware of how customers will use their products. Will it be for photos or videos? Will it play music? Or will it accomplish some other task?*

## DETERMINING WHAT IS NEEDED

The first step in the development of any software is to determine what the software needs to do. This information is rarely the result of pure guesswork. Instead, the software company gathers as much information as possible from potential customers. In order to do so, analysts determine who would be best to talk to and what questions to ask them. Perhaps one of the most important questions is, "Which features will be most important to the user?"

In the case of the Windows 10 operating system, Microsoft decided to focus on making sure it could work on a variety of devices. Developers worked on making sure Windows 10 could operate smoothly with both touch-screen devices and laptop computers. In addition, Microsoft listened to many of its customers' complaints and praises about previous operating systems. Then they made sure that Windows 10 reflected the strengths of those systems while easing away from the weaknesses.

# THE DRAWING BOARD

The next step for a development team is to lay down the big-picture outline for the software's creation. This stage requires a number of important decisions, which are often up to the software architect. One factor to be determined is how the program's various features will work. Another concerns how that program will operate within various systems. Will people be using it on certain types of phones? How will it work with Windows and Apple operating systems? Similar issues involve how the software will relate to other programs and connect with hardware elements.

One of the biggest challenges in software architecture is determining which elements of a program are most critical. These elements form the software's basic structure. Smaller features can be altered fairly easily later on, but the larger structural elements cannot.

One of the most significant architectural elements in Windows 10 is the ability to function with a range of Windows-based devices and systems. This addresses one of Windows 10's most important goals: being a universal hub for Windows applications.

*Computers today often run several programs at once. Many developers focus on making sure their new software can function in that environment.*

# WHERE THE MAGIC HAPPENS

*Some big technology companies, such as Apple, have headquarters that include a whole campus of buildings.*

## IT'S NOT EASY

Working in the computer industry can be challenging. At many companies, employees experience tremendous intensity, long hours, and sky-high expectations. There will be quiet times and times when you feel like pulling your hair out. However, software development jobs definitely have their perks.

## DEMANDING DEDICATION

At major companies such as Apple or Microsoft, 80-hour workweeks and little sleep are part of everyday life. Managers may e-mail an employee at 3:00 a.m. and expect a detailed reply within minutes. For many people, this means there is very little room left for a life outside the company. Companies that were born with the Internet, such as Amazon, Google, or Facebook, have similar high expectations. Some employees at Facebook, for example, spend a certain amount of time "on call." This means they can be called in to work at any time, day or night, to solve an issue.

# THE PAYOFF

The work can be rough, but it can also be rewarding. Big tech companies often offer a lot of perks. Lunch is one. Some of even the smallest companies employ caterers to prepare food each day. This food is often offered to employees for free. A range of foods may also be available for purchase, from vending machines to sit-down dining. Flexible work hours are another perk. A Microsoft employee who wants to work in the middle of the night can do that. He or she must simply be sure to get the job done and always be available for emergencies. Vacation time can also be easy to come by. For some companies, particularly small start-up companies, it is almost unlimited!

There is also the opportunity to work with some of the most brilliant minds in the tech industry. As you push yourself to greater heights, your own skills grow tremendously. Plus, being able to include a prestigious company in your resume almost guarantees employment elsewhere.

*Workers at Google have a range of seating options—including beanbag chairs!*

# FROM ABSTRACT TO CONCRETE

With the big-picture plan completed, it's time to decide all the little features that will go into that vision. It's a bit like a jigsaw puzzle. The finished puzzle forms a picture, but several separate pieces go into forming that picture. For example, every program has some kind of interface, or a process a person uses to control the program. Will it be a simple GUI with very few frills, or should it be prettier? Which features will be up front, available as soon as the program opens? Which features will be tucked away? What will each feature do, and how will the user go about launching it? Will the program be built more for speed or for quality performance? Will it honor previous or similar versions, or will it be entirely new?

Look at Microsoft's Windows 10 and ask yourself these types of questions. You may begin to see what the developers had in mind. The start menu, for example, uses both the "list" approach and the "tile" approach. This is a combination of Windows 7 and Windows 8 characteristics. It's a minor detail, but it represents Microsoft's larger vision for the new system: to combine elements from these two older systems.

*Windows 10's start menu combines the best elements of Microsoft's previous two operating systems.*

*Workers might adapt existing code to a new program or write it completely from scratch.*

## SO IT BEGINS

After all the prep work, the developers begin actually creating the program. This is when they slowly build on their computer screens what the user will eventually see. In some cases, a new product is built from scratch, essentially making something from nothing. In other instances, existing code from another program forms the foundation. This is often the case with software as complex as an operating system.

For Windows 10, programmers used existing code from an operating system called Windows NT, which first rolled out in 1993. Then they added or subtracted elements as needed. This is a lot less time-consuming than creating an operating system from the ground up. It also makes testing and debugging easier. This is because many functions and features were smoothed out long ago. Regardless, the programmers still need to watch for difficulties that could arise from the new features. Just because a line of code worked perfectly in Windows 7 or 8 doesn't mean it will work perfectly in 10.

# LASTING CONTRIBUTIONS

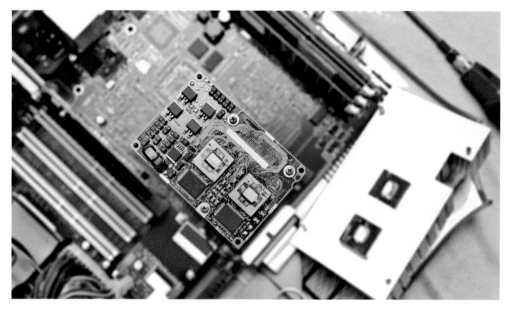

*A processor card might contain two or more microchips.*

## OUR LITTLE FRIEND THE MICROPROCESSOR

Many aspects of computer technology have evolved so far that they barely resemble what came before. Monitors, for example, went from displaying one color on a tiny screen to many intense colors and clarity on giant flat screens.

One element of the computer that has changed little, however, is the microprocessor. A microprocessor is basically a computer's "brain." It is a circuit that processes all or most of a computer's functions.

## FASTER AND FASTER

The microprocessor has been around for a while. One of the earliest was part of the System 21 computer, released by Viatron Computer Systems in 1968. The company Intel introduced its first microprocessor in 1971. It could process 4 bits, or binary digits, of code at a time. In 1978, the Intersil 16-bit microprocessor came out. It could process four times the bits as Intel's first unit. By the 1980s, there were 32-bit microprocessors. Sixty-four-bit units were used in businesses in the 1990s and in homes in the 2000s. These days, there are even faster "multicore" designs. There

*High-quality graphics, such as those used in many modern video games, require vast amounts of processing power.*

is still one chip, but it holds more than one microprocessor. These units have become popular, particularly with the rise of graphic-heavy games. Such programs require computers to draw detailed images more rapidly than ever.

## BIG BUSINESS

Roughly 12 billion microprocessors are produced every year. They foster an industry of tremendous growth and importance in the tech universe. And yet, the fundamental purpose of the processor has not changed since the beginning. It still makes sure both hardware and software work together in harmony. ✳

*Employees construct computer devices at a Sony factory in Wales.*

*By involving many people in the testing process, developers receive a wide range of opinions about a product.*

## UNDER THE MICROSCOPE

No matter how brilliant the engineers are, software must undergo testing throughout its development. In most cases, testing will be done not by one person, but by a whole team of people. Very often, those testers focus on just one aspect of the program at a time. For example, they might test to see if links between one aspect of an application and another work. They might also make sure any text is spelled correctly and makes sense. Even very basic programs can be tested from countless angles. The larger the software, the more complex the testing process is.

In the case of Windows 10, Microsoft had thousands of people running tests for years. The process wasn't limited to just Microsoft employees either. The company asked ordinary people to beta test the system at various stages of its development. This means they tried out a program that was nearing completion but not yet released. Beta testers reported any bugs they found or elements of the program they liked or disliked.

## MAKING SURE EVERYONE GETS ALONG

Another aspect of testing and QA involves making sure everything will work together. This includes all the parts to a program and the computer system the software will work within. Software also needs to work reliably with all other programs and any hardware connected to the same system. This is a critical phase in the development of a piece of software. Many programs may function smoothly when they are the only one on a system. But add the program to a system that has other programs, and it might crash.

With something as complex as an entire operating system, the process takes years. This proved to be one of the most difficult and time-consuming aspects of Windows 10's development. The operating system would be used by millions of people for countless purposes. It would have to work in a huge range of situations and with a huge variety of software and hardware.

*With so many different devices available, a program needs to be able to adapt to a range of systems.*

# GETTING IT OUT THERE

A company might spend many years and millions of dollars designing and testing great new software. Next comes the process of selling and distributing it. This is sometimes called the deployment phase. It can be one of the most challenging and important stages. First, the company officially announces the release of the product. Users then buy the product, install it on their computer, and activate it to start using it. These days, one of the most common ways customers access software is by downloading it from the Internet. People also often purchase it in some physical form, such as a CD or flash drive.

Even at this stage, there can be complications. A piece of software can receive the thumbs-up from its development team. However, customers often think differently. With Windows 10, many users with older versions of Windows had difficulty **upgrading** to the new version. In some cases, they decided to delete everything from their computers and do a fresh installation. Even then, they found snags with Windows 10's ability to communicate with older hardware. In some cases, frustrated users went back to their previous operating systems.

*A program might have trouble communicating with hardware such as printers when used in the real world. Users report these issues to the company, which works to fix the problem.*

*Some software designers work directly with users and fix issues in person.*

## WE'VE ONLY BEGUN

Once new software is released, the company that produced it must support and maintain it. They continue communicating with customers and rapidly respond to whatever problems arise. The customer feedback they receive will lead to a much better product down the line. It also guides the company toward better new products in the future. Each time a new bug is discovered, the developers must re-create what happened and find a solution. Then they offer the necessary fixes to the customers. When a program compiles enough of these fixes, the company may offer a downloadable "package." This package addresses all the fixes at once. Microsoft, for example, is famous for its service packs. These repair perhaps 50 to 100 little issues at one time. Companies often offer fully updated versions of a program, too. New customers then know the software has already gone through the refinement process.

In Windows 10, most bugs and their fixes occurred in the months immediately following the initial release. The same is true for any large-scale software. Companies hope that such a system will become smoother and more reliable as time passes. This was the case with Windows 7, which was why so many users regarded it so highly.

# THE FUTURE

Predicting the future of software and computer technology is no easy trick. There are, however, some signs of what the years ahead might hold.

## ALL ABOUT THE IMAGE

Graphics are becoming increasingly important to users. As a result, some experts expect the graphics processing unit (GPU), which processes the images on the screen, to become incredibly important. Advanced GPU technology is already being used in scientific, engineering, and other similar applications. It is likely only a matter of time before it's equally available in homes.

*GPUs release heat when in use and need fans to keep from overheating. Some GPUs are so powerful, they need more than one fan to stay cool.*

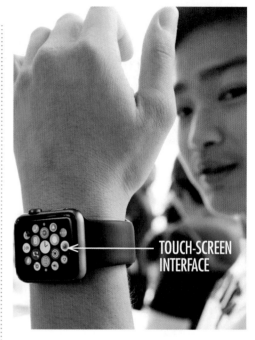

**TOUCH-SCREEN INTERFACE**

*The Apple Watch was released around the world in 2015.*

**PORTS CONNECT GPU TO MONITORS**

**FANS PULL HOT AIR OFF THE GPU**

## UNDERSTANDING DATA

There are awesome stores of information on hard drives around the world. But the average human mind can't accommodate all that information. Computers, however, can do just that. They process data to find patterns and draw conclusions of real, useful value. With this in mind, programmers are beginning to place more importance on

*Modern apps allow smartphones to communicate with computers on washing machines and other appliances.*

data-mining, or data-collecting, programs. They're also focusing more on database software, which turns the data into usable information.

## DEALING WITH DEVICES

Hardware is moving forward by leaps and bounds. Companies are not just working on making mobile phones and computers more powerful. They're also developing eyeglasses, watches, and televisions that can run programs and connect to the Internet. Vacuums, refrigerators, light switches, and even cars can be controlled via computers. All these devices require new, compatible software. The spread of sensor technologies, such as GPS, motion sensors, or heart rate monitors, has placed increasing demands on developers. New or updated software needs to be able to understand and work with these types of input.

There's no doubt the computer industry will grow and change. One aspect is likely to stick around, however. Humans will sit at that keyboard, gaze into that screen, and take the time to develop the software to make that growth possible.

# CAREER STATS

## SOFTWARE ENGINEERS

MEDIAN ANNUAL SALARY (2015): $93,000

NUMBER OF JOBS (2015): 1,000,000

PROJECTED JOB GROWTH (THROUGH 2017): 22%

PROJECTED INCREASE IN JOBS (THROUGH 2017): 200,000

REQUIRED EDUCATION: Bachelor's degree

LICENSE/CERTIFICATION: May be required for some positions; licensing generally not required

## COMPUTER PROGRAMMERS

MEDIAN ANNUAL SALARY (2015): About $75,000

NUMBER OF JOBS (2015): 350,000

PROJECTED JOB GROWTH (THROUGH 2017): 8%

PROJECTED INCREASE IN JOBS (THROUGH 2017): 30,000

REQUIRED EDUCATION: Bachelor's degree

LICENSE/CERTIFICATION: May be required for some positions; licensing generally not required

## COMPUTER SYSTEMS ANALYSTS

MEDIAN ANNUAL SALARY (2015): About $80,000

NUMBER OF JOBS (2015): 550,000

PROJECTED JOB GROWTH (THROUGH 2017): 25%

PROJECTED INCREASE IN JOBS (THROUGH 2017): 125,000

REQUIRED EDUCATION: Bachelor's degree

*Figures reported by the United States Bureau of Labor Statistics*

# RESOURCES

**BOOKS**

Diehn, Andi. *Technology: Cool Women Who Code*. White River Junction, VT: Nomad Press, 2015.

Gifford, Clive. *Awesome Algorithms and Creative Coding*. New York: Crabtree Publishing, 2015.

Greek, Joe. *A Career in Computer Graphics and Design*. New York: Rosen Publishing, 2015.

McManus, Sean. *How to Code in 10 Easy Lessons*. Lake Forest, CA: Walter Foster Publishing, 2015.

Payne, Bryson. *Teach Your Kids Code: A Parent-Friendly Guide to Python Programming*. San Francisco: No Starch Press, 2015.

Zizka, Theo. *3D Modeling*. North Mankato, MN: Cherry Lake Publishing, 2014.

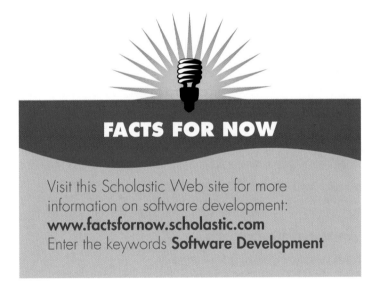

**FACTS FOR NOW**

Visit this Scholastic Web site for more information on software development:
**www.factsfornow.scholastic.com**
Enter the keywords **Software Development**

# GLOSSARY

**algorithm** (AL-guh-rih-thum) a set of steps for a computer to execute

**circuit** (SUR-kut) a two-way communication path between points

**code** (KODE) the instructions of a computer program, written in a programming language

**commands** (kuh-MANDZ) words or phrases that a user types to tell a computer program what to do

**cursor** (KUR-sur) a small indicator on a computer screen that shows where the computer's next action will take place

**hardware** (HAHRD-wair) computer equipment

**interface** (IN-tur-fase) the point at which two things meet; for example, a keyboard is one type of interface between a user and a computer

**languages** (LANG-wij-iz) in computers, the code in which instructions for a machine is written

**monitor** (MAH-ni-tur) the visual display screen of a computer

**operating system** (AH-pur-ay-ting SIS-tuhm) software in a computer or other device that supports all the programs that run on it

**optimization** (ahp-ti-mih-ZAY-shuhn) the process of making something as good or effective as possible

**protocol** (PROH-tuh-kawl) a set of rules about how information is moved among computers or over a network so that no information is lost

**software** (SAWFT-wair) computer programs that control the workings of the equipment, or hardware, and direct it to do specific tasks

**upgrading** (UHP-grayd-ing) replacing a computer part or a piece of software with a better, more powerful, or more recently released version

**vendor** (VEN-dur) a person or business that sells something

# INDEX

Page numbers in *italics* indicate illustrations.

# INDEX

# ABOUT THE AUTHOR

**WIL MARA** is the award-winning, best-selling author of more than 150 books, many of which are educational titles for children. He has held an intense interest in computer technology all his life, building his own home systems since the mid-1990s, participating in the beta testing of several Microsoft applications, and spending several years working as an editor and production manager at Prentice Hall's Professional Technical Reference division.